NO LONGER PROPERTY OF
THE SEATTLE PUBLIC

JUN 27 2014

Green Lake Library

Road Trip: Exploring America's Regions

LET'S EXPLORE THE

PACIFIC NORTHWEST

BY KATHLEEN CONNORS

Gareth Stevens
Publishing

Please visit our website, www.garethstevens.com. For a free color catalog of all our high-quality books, call toll free 1-800-542-2595 or fax 1-877-542-2596.

Library of Congress Cataloging-in-Publication Data

Connors, Kathleen.
  Let's explore the Pacific Northwest / Kathleen Connors.
      pages cm. — (Road trip: exploring America's regions)
  Includes index.
  ISBN 978-1-4339-9140-0 (pbk.)
  ISBN 978-1-4339-9141-7 (6-pack)
  ISBN 978-1-4339-9139-4 (library binding)
  1. Pacific States—Juvenile literature. I. Title. II. Title: Let us explore the Pacific Northwest.
  F851.C66 2013
  917.9504'44—dc23
                                                2012049206

First Edition

Published in 2014 by
Gareth Stevens Publishing
111 East 14th Street, Suite 349
New York, NY 10003

Copyright © 2014 Gareth Stevens Publishing

Designer: Andrea Davison-Bartolotta
Editor: Kristen Rajczak

Photo credits: Cover, p. 1 (left) AbleStock.com/Thinkstock, (right) Galyna Andrushko/Shutterstock.com; cover, back cover, interior backgrounds (texture) Marilyn Volan/Shutterstock.com; cover, back cover (map) Stacey Lynne Payne/Shutterstock.com; cover, back cover, pp. 1, 22–24 (green sign) Shutterstock.com; interior backgrounds (road) Renata Novackova/Shutterstock.com, (blue sign) Vitezslav Valka/Shutterstock.com; pp. 4, 5 (map, background), 11, 19 (yellow note), 21 iStockphoto/Thinkstock; p. 5 (curled corner) JonnyDrake/Shutterstock.com, (Canada map) Emir Simsek/Shutterstock.com; p. 6 Stas Moroz/Shutterstock.com; p. 7 mikenorton/Shutterstock.com; p. 8 Witold Skrypczak/Lonely Planet Images/Getty Images; p. 9 David McNew/Getty Images; p. 12 Joy Prescott/Shutterstock.com; p. 13 ML Harris/The Image Bank/Getty Images; p. 15 VanHart/Shutterstock.com; p. 16 Ingram Publishing/Thinkstock; p. 17 Stockbyte/Thinkstock; p. 19 margouillat photo/Shutterstock.com; p. 20 Paul Morigi/Getty Images.

All rights reserved. No part of this book may be reproduced in any form without permission in writing from the publisher, except by a reviewer.

Printed in the United States of America

CPSIA compliance information: Batch #CS13GS: For further information contact Gareth Stevens, New York, New York at 1-800-542-2595.

Contents

Words in the glossary appear in **bold** type the first time they are used in the text.

Heading Northwest

The Pacific Northwest has a rich history that dates back to Spanish explorers in the 1500s. It's one end of the famous Oregon Trail, too.

What are the borders of the Pacific Northwest? This is a matter of opinion. Geography, climate, and **culture** have all been used to decide the borders for the **region**. The states most often considered part of the Pacific Northwest are Washington and Oregon. Northern California, Idaho, and western Montana are commonly included, too.

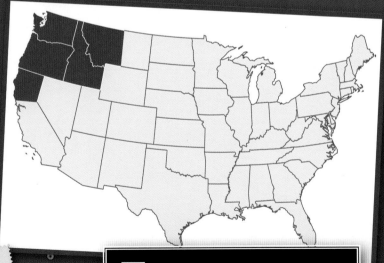

The Pacific Northwest

British Columbia

British Columbia, Canada, which shares a border with Washington, Idaho, and Montana, is often included in the Pacific Northwest, too. The states in this chart are those most commonly considered part of the region.

The Pacific Northwest
at a Glance

	State	Population (2010)	Date of Statehood	Capital	State Bird	State Flower
1	**California**	37,253,956	Sept. 9, 1850	Sacramento	California valley quail	California poppy
2	**Idaho**	1,567,582	July 3, 1890	Boise	mountain bluebird and peregrine falcon	Lewis's mock orange
3	**Montana**	989,415	Nov. 8, 1889	Helena	western meadowlark	bitterroot
4	**Oregon**	3,831,074	Feb. 14, 1859	Salem	western meadowlark	Oregon grape
5	**Washington**	6,724,540	Nov. 11, 1889	Olympia	willow goldfinch	coast rhododendron

Knowing the Land

The Pacific Northwest is such a hard area to define because of how different one part of it is from another. There are forests, deserts, mountains, and an ocean coast.

The Pacific Ocean to the west and the Rocky Mountains to the east are two of the main geographic features of the region. Additionally, the Pacific Northwest has 20 of the largest rivers in North America! This system of rivers reaches from southern Alaska to northern California.

Pit Stop

There are 17 national forests in Oregon and Washington, including Mount Hood National Forest in Oregon and Olympic National Forest in Washington.

While some use the Rocky Mountains as a natural eastern border of the Pacific Northwest, others include the Great Plains beyond the Rockies in the region, too.

Fiery Slopes

Have you ever seen an active **volcano**? You can visit two in the Pacific Northwest! Scientists believe either could **erupt** again in the near future.

Newberry National Volcanic Monument is part of Deschutes National Forest in central Oregon. Visitors can drive through the caldera, or large depression made by volcanic activity, of Newberry. There are cool rocks resulting from past eruptions everywhere!

Mount St. Helens erupted in 1980, destroying the forest around it. Today, it's a popular **destination** in southwest Washington—if a possibly dangerous one!

Newberry Volcano

Scientists keep a close watch on Newberry and Mount St. Helens. Constant observation will allow them to give lots of notice should either volcano seem ready to erupt.

Pit Stop

Even though Mount St. Helens is an active volcano, it's popular to climb! Climbers are asked to wear helmets in case rocks fly out of the crater. They also must be ready to leave quickly if conditions become dangerous.

The Sound and the River

Made up of deep-water harbors, streams, and islands, the Puget Sound is a great road-trip destination. Washington's cities of Seattle, Tacoma, and Olympia, among others, are found right on its shores. This makes the Puget Sound area home to about 60 percent of Washington's 6.8 million people! Visitors can tour the sound by boat and even go whale watching.

You can find the longest river that flows into the Pacific Ocean in the Pacific Northwest, too—the Columbia River!

Pit Stop

The Grand Coulee Dam was built in Washington on the Columbia River in the 1930s. Today, it's the largest producer of **hydroelectric** power in the United States.

The Columbia River Gorge runs through southern Washington and northern Oregon. It's full of hiking trails and beautiful scenery!

11

First Settlers

As in other regions of the United States, Native Americans lived in the Pacific Northwest long before European explorers or US settlers. Today, many tribes keep the history of their people alive through museums and tours of their communities and historic places, such as battlefields.

Tillicum Village is a popular attraction near Seattle, Washington. It's located on Blake Island, a place special to the Suquamish and Duwamish tribes. Visitors take a boat ride to the island and learn about Native American culture in the Pacific Northwest.

Blake Island

Native American tribes had to fight for their land in the Pacific Northwest. You can visit the locations of many of these battles today.

Pit Stop

Post

The tradition of carving totem poles began with Native American tribes living in Alaska and British Columbia. Though you can see totem poles throughout Washington State now, the first totem pole didn't come to Seattle until about 1900.

Seattle and Portland

No road trip through the Pacific Northwest is complete without a few days in Seattle, Washington! Catch a Mariners baseball game or visit the pop culture displays of the **interactive** EMP Museum. Head underground to explore streets—now tunnels—of a Seattle area that burned down in the 1800s. Parts of present-day Seattle are built over it!

Portland, Oregon, is the second-most-populous city in the Pacific Northwest, with more than 590,000 people. It's home to Powell's City of Books, a well-known bookstore, and the Oregon Zoo.

Pit Stop

Post

In 2012, Seattle's Space Needle turned 50! The famous landmark was built for the 1962 World's Fair. From its observation deck, visitors can spy Mount Rainier, Puget Sound, and the Cascade Mountains.

More than 620,000 people live in Seattle. It's the most populous city in the Pacific Northwest.

Rainy Days

On a road trip through the Pacific Northwest, bring a raincoat! Washington's Olympic Peninsula can have more than 150 inches (381 cm) of **precipitation** a year, and northwest California may have even more. The coast of Oregon also can be very wet. However, other areas of the region are quite dry.

Temperatures change from place to place, too. It may be only 50°F to 60°F (10°C to 16°C) in the Cascades in July, while Spokane, Washington, can top 100°F (38°C) during summer!

Pit Stop

The large stretch of sand dunes in Oregon has been millions of years in the making. At Oregon Dunes National Recreational Area, you can hike, camp, and watch the wind and water shape these special dunes.

Both the Pacific Ocean and the mountains of the Pacific Northwest greatly affect the weather of the area.

In a Northwest State of Mind

The Pacific Northwest is often **characterized** as more than a region—it's a way of living. Portland, Oregon, has been named the "greenest city in America" by several magazines, with Seattle not far behind. People from the region are well known for their concern for the **environment**.

Many groups in the Pacific Northwest, including the US Forestry Service, work to save wildlife in the region, too. From salmon to butterflies, you can learn a lot about wildlife **conservation** at the many national parks in the Pacific Northwest.

Pit Stop

Salmon, along with shellfish like clams and Dungeness crab, are a big industry for the Pacific Northwest and are commonly eaten there.

Applesauce

Ingredients:

4 apples with the cores cut out, peeled and chopped

3/4 cup water

1/4 cup white sugar

1/2 tsp ground cinnamon

Directions:

1. Mix all ingredients in a pot.

2. Cover the pot and let them cook together for about 20 minutes, or until the apples are soft.

3. Let the mixture cool.

4. Mash the mixture with a fork, or put in a blender to make the applesauce smooth.

Many kinds of apples and pears are grown in the Pacific Northwest. Ask an adult to help you follow these directions to make a tasty applesauce!

Famous Faces

Many successful and well-known people have come from the Pacific Northwest. Here's a list of a few big names who hailed from Seattle:

Chief Seattle (1790–1866): leader of tribes near Puget Sound who worked with settlers to establish land for his people. The city of Seattle is named for him.

Jimi Hendrix (1942–1970): famous guitar player. His grave in Renton, Washington, is popular with tourists.

Bill Gates (1955–present): cofounder of Microsoft. Microsoft's headquarters are near Seattle, too!

Bill Gates

Weird and Wonderful Pit Stops
in the
Pacific Northwest

Trees of Mystery
Klamath, California
An almost 50-foot (15 m) figure of
Paul Bunyan greets visitors to this trail
located in Redwood National Park.

Harvey the Giant Rabbit
Aloha, Oregon
Named after an imaginary rabbit in a
movie, this figure is 26 feet (8 m) tall!

Teapot Dome Gas Station
Zillah, Washington
This teapot-shaped gas station
was built in the 1920s.

Shortest River in the World
Great Falls, Montana
The Roe River is only about
200 feet (61 m) long!

Glossary

characterize: to point out features of

conservation: the care of the natural world

culture: the beliefs and ways of life of a group of people

destination: the place someone is traveling to

environment: the natural place in which a plant or animal lives

erupt: burst forth

hydroelectric: having to do with creating power by using the movement of water

interactive: having to do with the actions of a user

precipitation: rain, snow, sleet, or hail

region: an area

volcano: an opening in a planet's surface through which hot, liquid rock sometimes flows

For More Information

Books

Orr, Tamra. *Pacific Northwest Recipes.* Hockessin, DE: Mitchell Lane Publishers, 2012.

Sonneborn, Liz. *Northwest Coast Indians.* Chicago, IL: Heinemann Library, 2012.

Tieck, Sarah. *Oregon.* Minneapolis, MN: ABDO Publishing Company, 2013.

Websites

Pacific Northwest Native Americans
nativeamericans.mrdonn.org/northwest.html
Learn more about the Native American tribes that lived in the Pacific Northwest.

Ten Facts About the Pacific Northwest
geography.about.com/od/unitedstatesofamerica/a/pacificnorthwest.htm
Read some fun facts about this region of the United States.

Publisher's note to educators and parents: Our editors have carefully reviewed these websites to ensure that they are suitable for students. Many websites change frequently, however, and we cannot guarantee that a site's future contents will continue to meet our high standards of quality and educational value. Be advised that students should be closely supervised whenever they access the Internet.

Index